# THE walking BIRD
## collected words

M.F. GORDON

THE WALKING BIRD: COLLECTED WORDS
Copyright © 2021 M.F. Gordon
All rights reserved.

Cover art by Errol Mendoza
Typesetting and cover design by FormattingExperts.com

ISBN 978-1-5272-9467-7
Published by Alchemy Press

**DEDICATION**

For my Father
without whom
there would have been
no Pen.

## IN THE ABSENCE OF PURITY

I make
amends,
concede to
my mortality.
Wilfully stroke
my conceit
and ego,
to bolster
the reality
of my search
for surety,
in the absence
of purity.

**CLEARER TO SEE THROUGH**

I write
on sand.
It turns
to glass.
Clearer to
see through.

**HUMILITY**

Explicit to
human
is humility.
Everyone is one.

### THE WALKING BIRD

Shall I write
furiously
of success.
The hurt,
that reduces
my hands to
pinioned flesh.
Permits me
movement
neither way,
when all
the youth
around me
shout
their arrival
in strong coloured
visions of fame,
in the very things
I denounce,
pinch me with
their imbecility

till I bleed,
silently
from a desk.
Why the need
to paint a dot.
It will only
dry.
Crack with
a sharp sting
crumble,
following me
to earth.
Yet how
I am taunted
by a fact.
I have
the wings of
the flight,
I must become
the walking bird.

1963

## THE SNAKE IN THE GRASS

He tires.
No longer
admires
his prospects,
which he borrowed
so long ago,
from likes
and dislikes.
His responsibility,
that responded to
all but himself.
So he watches
as the light
grows dim,
the snake
in the grass
shed its skin.

## THAT I LIVED AND LOVED

I am
falling out
of love.
Help me
it hurts.
Rush me
to the nearest
memory,
but it is
fading
and smells
of stale sweat
from lust sweet
afternoons
spent in trust.
Deny me
anything,
but that
I lived
and loved.

## UNREQUITED LOVE

The sun
hangs crucified
in the sky.
The eye of
our universe
that will be
till the end.
The religion
that touches all
but cannot
in turn
be touched.
Indiscriminate.
Giving definition
to our solitude,
distance and
the comfort of
unrequited love.

## THE CHERRY TREE

After the
razzamatazz of
cherry blossom,
cherries.
Bold
and bright
then when
ripe, under
a spent sky,
we cherry pick.

### THE APPLE

The apple
doesn't fall
far from
the tree,
but some
trees are
on hills.

### FOREST

The forest
is hidden
by trees.
Bend
a little.
See the
flowers
growing.

## BOTTLED IN SCOTLAND

Youth
is the deity
we held
so briefly
with such
cavalier charm,
ruling our revels
without alarm.
Then age came.
Sunk in sobriety
glass in hand,
the memories
return,
bottled
in Scotland.

## THE CONDUCTRESS ON THE BLUEBIRD BUS

My first love
was for
the conductress on
the Bluebird bus.
I, at eleven
years old and
she at eleven
each morning,
came to Granny's
house for tea.
Red lipstick mouth,
brown curly hair
that begged
for touch.
Brown eyes which
laughed and
wrapped me up.
Her perfume made
me quite immobile.
My heart burst,
as I quietly
drank my tea,
as I wondered
dare I ask,
would she
wait for me.

## THE ROWAN TREE

As a child
I played under
the Rowan tree.
Forever trying
to touch
it's branches,
bend the berries
near to me.
Always
in my sight
never though
my reach.
Then one day
I climbed
the Rowan tree
and there inside,
found more berries
than I thought
could ever be.
Now I am
older,
can touch
its branches
but no longer
climb
the Rowan tree.

## IN A LAND SO FORLORN

I remember
margarine sandwiches
at the foot
of Cairn Gorm.
Midges biting
in drizzle dusk
and thinking
how exciting,
in a land
so forlorn.

## PASSING BY MY HOUSE

Too thin
the skin
that keeps me
from the elemental.
Two bricks thick.
No more
than ornamental.
I smile
with disbelief.
Passing by
my house.

### WHAT USE VANITY

What use
vanity.
It covers up
a lonely sin.
A mirror,
that touches
only skin.

### STING

The bee
can only
sting,
when you
can hear
the beating
of its
wings.

## WORDS PRONOUNCED DIFFERENTLY

The woman
snaps.
We have
nothing
in common.
The man
breaks.
We share
the same
weakness,
pronounced differently
spelt the same.
The woman cries
of love.
The man replies
with words
pronounced differently
spelt the same.

## IN ENGLISH

I cannot
hold you
forever
without speaking.
My soul
is not mute
but lonely,
as your body
remains a body.
Lust is burnt
for warmth.
My sight
is relinquished.
What is lost.
What language
do we speak
that celebrates
such anonymity.
Tolerates plural
in such singular
fashion.
Admires passion
in Latin
yet denies
confession,
in English.

## SEPARATE CORNERS

We have
painted
ourselves
into a corner.
Separate corners.
Lips move.
The distance is
too far to
hear our cries.
The paint
still sticky to
the touch.
Paint dries.

### SO SLIGHT

Distracted
by people
our loneliness
survives.
Our being
alone
only witnessed
by the night.
Where truth
moves you
closer to me
and I to you.
Cradling life.
A move
so slight.

## ANOTHER YEAR

Water
under the bridge.
The flow
of memories,
dancing like
diamonds
in the sun.
The river bed,
still not dry.

**FIRST LANGUAGE**

Words
disguise me
My disguise
is fluent.
My first language
forgotten.

**OVER**

Over the hill
lies that
which already
exists.
I made
far too many
detours.

## A SLOW SUMMER DAY

A slow
summer day
making snails
of us all.
Caught by
the air.
Watching
breathless butterflies
prancing and
dancing,
in delight of
the light.

## WHILE WALKING WITH LUDO

I remember
such days
when the sun
spilt out of
the sky.
Lit up
my eyes
with warmth
of being
alive.
Its breath
in time to
my heart.
With no
reason for
reason.

## SWEET JAZZ MAN

There is
a weariness,
heavy as heat
on a summer day,
which only knows
relief with night.
A weight removed.
The Jazzman,
silhouetted
by light,
picks out
by sound
the soul.
Leaving in the air
sweet Jazz man.

## I SIT WITH MY FRIEND

The sun
spotted me
as I casually
strolled through
my youth.
Then later, not
so much later.
Bridges burnt,
the world done.
I sit with
my friend
and remember.

## A SIMPLE TRUTH

A blackbird
sings
a song
so pure
it cuts the air,
sets free
the heart.
We have left
behind
sense of place.
Years pass
without a trace
or is it that, in
all our doing,
then becomes
our own undoing.
Hides
a simple truth.
We are a part,
not apart.
A place
to free
the heart.

**DIRTY LINEN**

> The truth
> is too
> loose to
> handle.
> So we
> mangle
> our dirty
> linen.

**TAKEN FOR GRANTED**

> A bird
> in hand
> can fly
> to the
> bush.

**REPETITION**

The day
unfolds
in comfortable
repetition.
My discomfort
comes from
recognition
that no matter
what the will,
repetition
kills.

**SENTIMENT**

Sentiment
is a place
of longing.
Romantic
rhetoric.
Revisiting
something
that seemed
of worth.
A lost
belonging.

## DANGEROUS

Dangerous,
to let
a man
stand alone
too long.
To let him
see what's
gone wrong.
That all
his doing
to and fro,
rather spoils
the way
he grows.
To have him
find that,
the necessity
he weaves and
wears as
wedded bliss,
like confetti is
pretty pointless.

## A VERY BAD HABIT

Arrogance
suffers from
fear.
Offers up
as defence
a fine pretence.
Disdain
is commonplace
upon this
face,
light with
it's promise
of intent,
as are all
malcontents.
Arrogance
suffers from
fear,
then becomes
a habit.
Some people
have a very
bad habit.

## SOME CONSIDERABLE TIME

If I sit
here
long enough,
staring at
nothing,
it will become
reality,
which is
circumstance
that can be
changed
and I will
have been
wasting
some considerable
time.

**COMPROMISE**

To the
acceptor
there must
be given,
hope.
The compromise
of time.

**NOT DOING**

Waiting.
Left alone.
Not doing.
I see life
improving.

## LIKE A CHESHIRE CAT

The cats
confidence
struts ahead,
with faint
menace.
An air of
authority.
Doubt is out.
But cats
don't work.
I go upstairs.
Change.
Don my authority.
Return
smiling,
like a
Cheshire cat.

## A GIRLS' BLOUSE

Sitting in
a coffee house,
I saw a girls
breasts
burst through
her blouse.
Then again,
maybe not.
More, the
stretching of
the fabric
of my
imagination.

## WITHOUT A BROLLY

Life is
very jolly,
but in Britain
bring a
brolly.
The rain
is such
a pain,
drowning our
poor drains
and
goodness gracious
golly,
life is wet
without a
brolly.

## A FINE KETTLE OF FISH

I make
demands,
that are
in truth
demanded
of me,
by what
I allow
and
disallow.
Which in turn
is all
I am allowed
by my
imagination,
which is
imagined.
Leaving me,
steaming
with what
is left of
indignation.
A fine kettle
of fish
that I am
boiling in.
Please,
turn me down
to simmer.

## THE FINAL FURLONG

Let me be,
with the
final furlong,
free from
fillies.
But no.
Silly billy,
my best
friend
William said.

**GIVEN TIME**

The richness
of memory
far outweighs
the poverty
of grief.
Given time.

**TIME**

Past
and future
are present.
Time
the measure
of man.

## SLEEPING IN PUBLIC

I feel
threatened,
as you
lie there.
A rude
awakening.
Seeing you,
sleeping
in public.
Your homeless
body
is too close
for comfort
or compassion.
Wrapped
in old news
for warmth,
while I carry
todays'
and grow cold,
feeling how
near you are
to me.

## BLOOD DRIPS

Blood runs
in my body.
So silent is
it's whisper
that I forget
its presence.
How necessary
this indifference is
for us
to live
and how
diffident
the reminder
that from
time to time,
blood drips.

## SPILT LEMON JUICE

Everything stops.
So suddenly.
I feel myself
staring at
myself.
A stranger.
Why am I here?
Where is here?
A nano second
if that.
The heart not
even finished
a single
beat.
The words have
disappeared.
A sheet of
blank paper.
Spilt lemon juice
perhaps.

Displaced.
Times too
I hear my
name called.
Why?
Who is calling me?
For what reason?
Yet I know why
and whom
and their reason.
Another blank
sheet of paper.
Spilt lemon juice
perhaps.
Displaced.
Then back again
to continue with
my aged bliss.
The comfort of
the story.

### LOOK AT ME

Centres collide
as we walk
the streets.
Strategies
in thin disguise,
hide behind those
vacant eyes.
Reveal what
cannot be
concealed.
A loneliness,
embarrassed by
a simple plea.
Look at me.

## MEMORIES

My memories
are stories
hidden away,
waiting for
a rainy day.
My desires
that grew tired.
The innocence
that survived.
And now
in pouring rain,
I see
distant land
I must reclaim.

**STILL LIFE**

Many pictures
capture me.
I recognise
most, yet
I still have
movement.
Still life.

**CONTENTMENT**

Not all
problems
need be
solved,
contentment
need not
lay with
burden of
proof.

## INSIDE THIS PRIMAL SCREAM

Escaped souls
howl
in the wind.
As I, safely
in my body,
walk with
quickened
step and
slapping feet
on wet slab
streets,
lit by yellow
lights
bare and indiscreet.
Torn by rain
upon my face
that falls off
flintstone walls
that creep along
like dinosaurs.
I dare not
look back,
so continue on
alone,
unseen.
Inside this primal
scream.

## A COMMON CALL

The sky
cries
freely
on earth.
Running in
streams and seas.
Feeding the
urgent need
of land
where we stand,
too often
dry, desperate
with those
demands
we make
of man.
Our souls,
damned
to bursting point,
when one tear
could give
balm to all.
Connect us with
a common call.

## THE PREDILECTION OF MAN

Reeling
in and out
the lines
beneath
the surface,
a fisherman
stands.
Seeing shadows.
Catching only
the tide
that turns
one way,
then the other.
His reflection
casts him
with affliction.
The predilection
of man.

## IN THE MIRAGE OF THE MIND

Delusion.
Illumination
ill-conceived.
A chance
to be deceived,
that once taken
leaves
a darkness,
where only anger
breathes.
Separate man
from kind
and we wander,
in the mirage
of the mind.

## A GRAIN OF SAND

A grain of
sand,
covered by
a thousand others
slips through
my fingers.
I have lost it
without knowing
where.
The sun stares
down on me,
as I demand
to understand
define
this loss,
then turns
drops
beneath horizon.
Extinguished
by dusk.
Beyond
my reach.
Defying
my conceit.
Like the grain
of sand,
its symmetry
complete.

**LIFE**

I only left
it for
a minute
and it
was gone

**PROOF**

Living
is
live
enough.
The living
proof.

## CONSTANT

I celebrate.
Not the
years
that pass,
each as
a blink of sun
at end of day.
Unnoticed.
Rather,
you and I.
Constant
in an
inconstant
world.

## THE SAME SUN

When apart
the heart
falters.
Something
not quite
there.
Memories
stare back,
return to
when we met.
The same sun
shines
as then.
I see it
shining now.

## A TOUCH

Doubt will
turn us
inside out.
Those failings,
that we
perceive as
self,
then eagerly
transfer to
others.
A loneliness
which will
not leave,
until an
outstretched hand.
A touch.

## CERTAINTY

Have we lost
that certainty
we held
in the stillness
and the dark?
We built our Ark.
Some time
has passed.
Was it really us?
Then I catch
its perfume.
Strong, sweet.
As like
a flower.

## JUST THERE

You lie
indolently,
over the arm
of the chair,
conducting Bach
in the air.
I sit feeling
safer,
having you
just there.

## WOMEN DO NOT START WARS

Women
do not
start wars.
Men do.
Women
bear witness,
are the
scabbard
for the
sword.

## NEWS

Tell me
the news.
What?
Somebody is
killing
somebody.
Ah!
The body
of news.

## FILLING IN TIME

Between
beginning
and end
there is
the middle.
I can count
my footsteps.
Sit in the sun
with dreams
all around.
Do good
in the world
or bad.
Whatever I do
is filling in
time.
A truth
which allows
for body
and mind.

## CHOICE

There is
no space.
None.
All is
occupied.
Filled in.
Circumstance
dictates.
Choice sets
free.
The choice
to enjoy,
despite
circumstance.

**ETERNITY**

Does
the blind man
see
eternity,
which is
hidden from
sight,
or is it
our very
last thought
frozen?
It is
nothing
that I can
understand.

## THE DEVIANCE THAT IS OUR SOUL

Genes will
out.
I am
a copycat.
I catch
myself in
mid-gesture
of my father
as he did his.
There is a
sense in this.
A copy
of a copy
translates life
as hope,
that never
dies.
Yet, it is
the difference
that still
persists
is past control,
the deviance
that is
our soul.

## INFINITY

Some
clever people
say
that at
the end,
the body
stops
then rots.
There is
no divinity.
Then what
of infinity,
which is
far beyond
belief or
mans' conceit.
Space
to keep
the soul.

## A ONE-NIGHT STAND

His clothes
lay by
the bed.
Rumpled, with
the urgency of
a one-night stand.
Morning comes,
with warmth
and indifference
to the night.
She stares
at him
in sad reproach.
What all men want.
He says goodbye
with lies.
Was good.
Will call,
then scurries
down the hall.
Not knowing,
yet knowing
that this
is not
what he wants
at all.

## TOO LATE

Loose language
escapes.
Scrapes
the gate
and with it
fate.
Then the
cry.
Too late.

## HOLDING MY BREATH

Holding my
breath
I count
the seconds
then let go.
Holding love,
it's absence
or life itself,
I count
the seconds
then let go.

## CONQUISTADOR

I carry
your worry
by proxy.
Love is no
dove.
Your vote
of confidence
results in
my diffidence.
You deceive
yourself.
I cannot
help.
Nor can I
turn
conspirator.
I will not
be your
Conquistador

## THE WARMTH OF PROMISE

When you
undress
or dress,
as if I'm
not a man.
Kiss with
lips that
barely touch.
What am I
to understand
of this.
This place.
Now space.
Yet love
lingers.
The warmth
of promise
covers
the cold
rationale
of time.

**ADVICE**

The vice
of
opinion.

**ONIONS**

Opinions
are like
onions.
Peel away
the first layer
to reveal
the next.
Ad infinitum.
Ad nauseam.
Onions
make me cry.

## MISS HELLO

Miss hello
is three years
old.
Smiling
from a face
without
a trace of
guile.
Complete
with fresh milk
teeth and
tricycle,
which soon
will be a
bicycle.
Then the cycle
will begin.
She'll grow
and grow
and grow.
Until it's time
for me
to say,
goodbye to
Miss Hello.

## MY OLD FACE HAS ARRIVED

How many
lines
can gather on
one face?
Sun
still smiles
from my eyes.
Excitement
of the unknown
still lingers,
though Sat Nav
now required
to find
those eyes.
My old face
has arrived.

## BATHROOM DOOR UNLOCKED

Lying
in my bath.
Staring at
my feet.
I try to feel
connected.
There is
a distance though,
encouraged by
my nakedness.
Without
my finery,
I am reduced
to mortal.
Safer then with
bathroom door
unlocked.

## THE BANK POEM

This account
is spent
and overdrawn.
A capital
investment,
which by
divestment
became
withdrawn.
Interest remains
on loan.

## MERE MALE

Sex
has been
called
a twitch
in the groin.
Fine.
But please.
Do I need
a hernia?
When
my meagre mind
a million
miles away,
contemplates
the mediocrity
of life,
though relieved
I still
identify,
I feel a twitch.
Oh if only

I could switch
to eunuch power!
On a bus.
Innocent
as my mother
intended,
or at work
with belief
in life
suspended.
I feel a twitch.
Will this
bitch twitch
ever cease?
It is
far beyond
the pale.
I am
after all
mere male.

**CONFIDENCE**

Confidence
is a
trick.
Now you
see it.
Now you
don't.

**DIFFERENCE**

The agreement
of doubt,
which leaves
no one out.

**RESPECT**

To gain
respect,
you must
first
give respect.
A silent
communion.

**RACISM**

Racism
is a pigment
of imagination.
Life
is coloured,
by people.

## THE TURQUOISE COAST

I heard
echoes of
wild horsemen,
racing across
the hills
that time had
left behind.
The sea
was fused
with sky.
Such a blue
that drew
my eyes
to only there.
As the sun
reached down,
scattered
diamonds
everywhere.
The myth
released.

## NORTH OF ALICE

In the dream time
the land sleeps.
To be awakened
by the rain.
The bare
red rubbed sand
lies hidden,
under a furious
confusion of flowers,
their colours rush
to celebrate
along with
pale green grass.
Beneath the sun
and stretched
blue sky,
in the silent heat.
I watch the earth
compete.

## IN THE STILLNESS

In the stillness,
the sky
at mid-day
stands in silence,
hardly breathing.
The sun beats
the earth,
my skin
and bones.
I wait.
The trees,
huddled together
in green
conspiracy,
wait.
The hills
wander
to a standstill,
wait.
All wait
in this
cathedral state.
Slowly,
the soldier sun
retreats,
admits
defeat.

## WHAT WE HAVE IN COMMON

The sun
flushed hotly
as it
climbed to noon.
Beneath,
covered by canvas
that smelt of
dried rain,
I slept.
Outside,
on bare
brown baked stone,
the snake slept.
I arose
as the sun fell,
just in time
to see its
red black back
slither away,
leaving me
standing there.
Quietly sharing,
what we have
in common.

## ALONE

How lonely
is alone.
As a stone
thrown
to the sea,
without
a ripple.

## SAD MAN

Sad man,
sitting
at a bar.
Belly pregnant
with expectation.
Never fulfilled.
Only refilled,
glass after glass.

## POEM FOR PENNY

Sometimes,
when
the sunlight
strokes your eyes
with obscene
familiarity,
your youth
is lost
to truth.
A harmless
occupation this,
of time
passing.
Life
should not be held
as some
porcelain dish,
more
the sum
of all
we wish.

## NOW AND THEN

Not now
but then,
when love caught
my breath
with every word
you said.
A sun
that never slept.
Life interrupts.
The tree
grows old.
Yet the leaves
remain
a dappled green.
Love is seen
in glimpses,
now and then.

## DEJA-VU

Let the
colours
fade not too
fast, or
voices be so
distant
as to not
be heard.
To disavow,
take as granted
the past
which we
passed through,
reduces all
to deja-vu.

## DISCARDED DREAMS

Memory recalls
discarded dreams.
Those very
dreams
which made us
once
so much alive.
A point to
all this living.
Is it not
a kindness then
to allow them
to survive.

**PERSPECTIVE**

If I reach
up with
stretched
fingers,
feel the air.
Am I not
touching
the sky?

**SOMETHING**

Nothing is
impossible.
There is
always
something.

**DANCE**

Let the
world
spin.
Listen to
its tune
and dance.

## THE VANISHING POINT

Youth bursts
unfettered as
laughter
from the soul.
No abyss here.
Rather an excitement,
shared by
glorious apprehension
of the unknown.
Pursuing forever
the vanishing point,
with such
glorious indiscretion
until that last
indiscretion,
when youth
is lost,
replaced by
a slow smile.

## WALKING ON AIR

The art
of youth is
impressionism.
Sitting at
a table
sunk in some
cellar,
listening to
senses
being played by sax.
Coughing on cigarettes.
Bits of breath.
Deeply intense
you play solitaire,
while chasing
cheap scent
of perfumed girls
passing past.
Tired of it all
you climb
the stairs
go out
on the street,
where people stare.
As you resume
walking on air.

## LET ME STAND BARE

Rip up
the streets.
There is
earth
beneath.
Strip me
of clothes,
leave me
exposed.
Collect from
my mind
my intellect.
Dispose
and forget.
Let me be
rare,
endangered.
Let me stand
bare.

**WAITING UNTIL THE WAR BEGINS**

Life
was expectation.
Mulling over moves
in anticipation.
Being lost
and found
then lost again.
Bemused
and then
accused.
The cardinal sin.
Waiting
until the war
begins.

## PEACE

There is
a need
to fill in time.
Life has become
far too
boring.
Lets have a drama.
Nothing
that makes any
real demand
you understand.
War, carnage pillage.
Mindless mayhem,
that sort of thing.
Something
of human interest,
with all that brings.
Then,
when that too
becomes too boring,
return to peace.
Any peace
we can get
from the pieces.

**DEATH**

All
this
fuss
over
nothing.

**UNSEEMLY**

Death
unravels.
Marvel
at the
unseemly
scrabble.

## PANDEMIC

Days
have become
impartial.
That of value
devalued.
And that it
could happen
between breaths.
The story line
broken.
Then stories
are a fiction.
Life holds
no such
restriction.

## THE LAMB

The selfish gene
is for
survival.
Persistent and insistent.
As was
my pursuit of
heedless fun
when young.
Now I see
so much
I missed,
which lay
in front
now lies
behind.
Yet
so much more
would I
have missed,
had not I
been naïve.
The lamb
with
lion's mane.

## MORALITY

Morality
is a corruption
of convenience.
Excused by
rationale.
Dependent on
immorality
for credibility.
A prerequisite
exquisite to
humanity.

**IN MY OWN PRESENCE**

> The past
> refuses
> to compensate
> the present.
> Future
> withholds its
> recompense.
> The only sense
> is now,
> as I stand
> in my own
> presence.

**NOWHERE ELSE**

Not fully
at first
merely a hint,
but eventually
its there,
for all to see.
Nowhere else
to hide.
The eyes
catch up
with the soul.

## ON GROWING OLDER

Bracing stuff
this growing
older.
So embrace.

## HUMOUR

Old age
is savage
yet gentle,
with the
humour
of time.

## WOOD

With age
comes
weathered skin
that storms
across the face.
The body leaks.
Memory leaves
reason elsewhere
and all veneer
is stripped back
to natural
wood.

## ALL STILL NEW

Old age
takes time.
Memory,
no time at all.
Serves well
the old,
as they recall
the child.
When memories
were few
and all
still new.

**AUTUMN**

The leaves
fall
bruised
and bright,
cartwheel
to earth,
in the warmth
of a sun
stolen from
a summer day.

**DAFFODILS**

Money
is second nature
to the rich.
All those
movers and
shakers.
Counting coins,
when they
could be
spending time
with
daffodils.

**SEX EXPLAINS**

Sex explains
everything.
Sorry.
I've got
a headache.

**A POINT OF VIEW**

How lonely
the point
of view,
that leaves
no room
for others.

### IT'S TIME FOR BED

I remember
a room
that wore
wallpaper
too thin
for decency.
The lilt
of voices
that would tilt
my world
into happiness,
as the rain
flung itself
furiously
against the window,
in tearful frustration.
And I glowed
warmly
in the shadow of
the tilley lamp,
that hissed
liked a snake.
Safe

from the sky
at dusk,
so blood red
I thought it dead.
Safe
from the Tinkers
who would surely
take me away,
or so I'd heard.
Cowering
with pleasure,
as the fire
leapt
into my eyes,
into caves
where buried treasure
danger lay
and every minute
must be saved.
Until my mother,
arm around me
softly said,
it's time for bed.

## ALL IN THE HOPES OF BEING WISE

Upon
the grassy slopes
I walk
with chanting cries
in front.
Birds burst forth
with friendly squawk
as I ascend
their mount.
Fear not
my little friends
no harm
can I foretell,
make your voices
happy blend
and a story tell.
As in front
the mountain rise,
down beneath
the valley lies,
this is the place
for idle tries
all in the hopes
of being wise

1958

# POEMS

| | |
|---|---:|
| IN THE ABSENCE OF PURITY | 1 |
| CLEARER TO SEE THROUGH | 3 |
| HUMILITY | 3 |
| THE WALKING BIRD | 4 |
| THE SNAKE IN THE GRASS | 7 |
| THAT I LIVED AND LOVED | 9 |
| UNREQUITED LOVE | 11 |
| THE CHERRY TREE | 13 |
| THE APPLE | 15 |
| FOREST | 15 |
| BOTTLED IN SCOTLAND | 17 |
| THE CONDUCTRESS ON THE BLUEBIRD BUS | 19 |
| THE ROWAN TREE | 21 |
| IN A LAND SO FORLORN | 23 |
| PASSING BY MY HOUSE | 25 |
| WHAT USE VANITY | 27 |
| STING | 27 |
| WORDS PRONOUNCED DIFFERENTLY | 29 |
| IN ENGLISH | 31 |
| SEPARATE CORNERS | 33 |
| SO SLIGHT | 35 |
| ANOTHER YEAR | 37 |
| FIRST LANGUAGE | 39 |
| OVER | 39 |
| A SLOW SUMMER DAY | 41 |
| WHILE WALKING WITH LUDO | 43 |
| SWEET JAZZ MAN | 45 |
| I SIT WITH MY FRIEND | 47 |
| A SIMPLE TRUTH | 49 |

| | |
|---|---:|
| DIRTY LINEN | 51 |
| TAKEN FOR GRANTED | 51 |
| REPETITION | 53 |
| SENTIMENT | 55 |
| DANGEROUS | 57 |
| A VERY BAD HABIT | 59 |
| SOME CONSIDERABLE TIME | 61 |
| COMPROMISE | 63 |
| NOT DOING | 63 |
| LIKE A CHESHIRE CAT | 65 |
| A GIRLS' BLOUSE | 67 |
| WITHOUT A BROLLY | 69 |
| A FINE KETTLE OF FISH | 71 |
| THE FINAL FURLONG | 73 |
| GIVEN TIME | 75 |
| TIME | 75 |
| SLEEPING IN PUBLIC | 77 |
| BLOOD DRIPS | 79 |
| SPILT LEMON JUICE | 80 |
| LOOK AT ME | 83 |
| MEMORIES | 85 |
| STILL LIFE | 87 |
| CONTENTMENT | 87 |
| INSIDE THIS PRIMAL SCREAM | 89 |
| A COMMON CALL | 91 |
| THE PREDILECTION OF MAN | 93 |
| IN THE MIRAGE OF THE MIND | 95 |
| A GRAIN OF SAND | 97 |
| LIFE | 99 |

| | |
|---|---|
| PROOF | 99 |
| CONSTANT | 101 |
| THE SAME SUN | 103 |
| A TOUCH | 105 |
| CERTAINTY | 107 |
| JUST THERE | 109 |
| WOMEN DO NOT START WARS | 111 |
| NEWS | 111 |
| FILLING IN TIME | 113 |
| CHOICE | 115 |
| ETERNITY | 117 |
| THE DEVIANCE THAT IS OUR SOUL | 119 |
| INFINITY | 121 |
| A ONE-NIGHT STAND | 123 |
| TOO LATE | 125 |
| HOLDING MY BREATH | 125 |
| CONQUISTADOR | 127 |
| THE WARMTH OF PROMISE | 129 |
| ADVICE | 131 |
| ONIONS | 131 |
| MISS HELLO | 133 |
| MY OLD FACE HAS ARRIVED | 135 |
| BATHROOM DOOR UNLOCKED | 137 |
| THE BANK POEM | 139 |
| MERE MALE | 140 |
| CONFIDENCE | 143 |
| DIFFERENCE | 143 |
| RESPECT | 145 |
| RACISM | 145 |
| THE TURQUOISE COAST | 147 |
| NORTH OF ALICE | 149 |
| IN THE STILLNESS | 151 |

| | |
|---|---:|
| WHAT WE HAVE IN COMMON | 153 |
| ALONE | 155 |
| SAD MAN | 155 |
| POEM FOR PENNY | 157 |
| NOW AND THEN | 159 |
| DEJA-VU | 161 |
| DISCARDED DREAMS | 163 |
| PERSPECTIVE | 165 |
| SOMETHING | 167 |
| DANCE | 167 |
| THE VANISHING POINT | 169 |
| WALKING ON AIR | 171 |
| LET ME STAND BARE | 173 |
| WAITING UNTIL THE WAR BEGINS | 175 |
| PEACE | 177 |
| DEATH | 179 |
| UNSEEMLY | 179 |
| PANDEMIC | 181 |
| THE LAMB | 183 |
| MORALITY | 185 |
| IN MY OWN PRESENCE | 187 |
| NOWHERE ELSE | 189 |
| ON GROWING OLDER | 191 |
| HUMOUR | 191 |
| WOOD | 193 |
| ALL STILL NEW | 195 |
| AUTUMN | 197 |
| DAFFODILS | 199 |
| SEX EXPLAINS | 201 |
| A POINT OF VIEW | 201 |
| IT'S TIME FOR BED | 202 |
| ALL IN THE HOPES OF BEING WISE | 205 |

www.ingramcontent.com/pod-product-compliance
Lightning Source LLC
Chambersburg PA
CBHW071159070526
44584CB00019B/2849